Nancy –
All.

RMJ DONALD LLC

Fine Books and Plays

PO Box 8 • Barrington • NH 03825

SHOULDERS

Also by Jeffrey Kinghorn from:

RMJ DONALD LLC
Fine Books and Plays

Plays
Shoulders
In a Coal Burning House

Ted Mitchell Detective Novels
Inside the Loop
The Cutter
1-800-Forgive

Novel for Young Readers
When We Were Happy

Honoring my parents,

Robert Henry and *Marie Jane*

— well done —

SHOULDERS

Shoulders
Jeffrey Kinghorn

Characters

Rosemary McClintock
Mother of Lorraine and Linda

Lorraine McClintock
Shipyard Welder

Linda McClintock
Teenager

Harriet Winston
Cab Driver

Natsuko Takimoto
Japanese-American

Salvatore Pasquaneri
Failed Gangster

Time
February/March, 1942

Setting
The McClintock back yard in San Francisco

One

February, 1942. Midnight. Abundant moonlight.

The back yard of a San Francisco bungalow. A covered porch. A screen door. Mis-matched yard furniture. Eucalyptus, Juniper, and Palm.

The world is at war. All people of Japanese descent on the Pacific Coast must report for internment.

At Rise:

LORRAINE, a stunning beauty in a strapless evening gown, enters from around the house to a spot perfect for watching the moon. Her luminous skin and the diamonds at her neck nullify the blackout.

SAL enters. He is dressed to the nines and carries her mink wrap. He is arrested at the sight of Lorraine in the moonlight. He approaches and drapes the mink over her shoulders.

LORRAINE turns for a kiss marked by tenderness and yearning.

Sal: (*Of the kiss*) Let me die now.

Lorraine: (*Of the moon*) Beautiful.

Sal: Come with me.

Lorraine: It looks so small.

Sal: Marry me, Lorraine.

Lorraine: Think we'll ever get there?

Sal: I'll give you anything you want.

Lorraine: What if I said I wanted the moon?

Sal: I'd figure a way.

Lorraine: I stand here every chance I get just to feel it on my skin.

Sal: Be my wife.

> *LORRAINE lets the mink slide off her shoulders. She moves about the yard.*
>
> *SAL picks up the mink and itches to embrace her again.*

2

LORRAINE stays just out of reach.

Lorraine: You haven't said a word about my dress.

Sal: Love the dress. Nuts about it.

Lorraine: Tomorrow night it's Jane's.

Sal: Crazy about the dame *in* the dress.

Lorraine: After her, it goes to Ann. Then Dierdre. Then Barbara. We call it the *Liberty Dress*. Cost a fortune.

Sal: I'll buy you all the dresses you'll ever want.

Lorraine: I like buying things for myself. (*Of the dress*) Part of them anyway.

Sal: Such a simple word *yes*.

Lorraine: I'm not quite myself in this dress.

Sal: You're killing me here.

Lorraine: You're the only man who has ever asked me to marry him.

Sal: The world is full of fools.

Lorraine: There have been no other men in my life.

Sal: Criminal.

Lorraine: My life never reached much beyond this yard. It used to be filled with clotheslines. You're the first man ever to step foot back here without an armload of laundry to drop off or to pick up.

Sal: Here I am with a handful of mink.

Lorraine: I wanted you to see it. This is what I am. What I come from.

Sal: Beautiful.

Lorraine: I could make supervisor next month. If I keep my hours up.

Sal: Forget about the shipyard. Come with me. You won't have to work.

Lorraine: All I've ever known is work.

Sal: You promised an answer tonight.

Lorraine: Yes. I know.

Sal: I haven't slept for days. I don't eat. Can't think.

Lorraine: You've been very patient.

Sal: Not exactly my strong suit.

Lorraine: I love it when you ask me.

> *SAL approaches and whispers in
> her ear.*

Sal: Marry me, Lorraine.

Lorraine: You've made me feel…beautiful.

Sal: Be my wife.

Lorraine: All the things young girls dream about.

Sal: Say yes.

Lorraine: I haven't been able to sleep either.

Sal: Let me hear it.

Lorraine: I thought surely I was going to say yes.

Sal: (*Beat*) Take your time. Don't rush.

Lorraine: I'm trying to use my head, not just my heart.

Sal: Already I don't like the sound a this.

Lorraine: I can't leave my mother and sister. I'm all they've got.

Sal: I'll take care of them.

Lorraine: My job.

Sal: What are you talkin about? You won't have to work!

Lorraine: I wouldn't know how not to work.

Sal: Get a job in Chicago. I'll put you on at the plant. Work for me.

The back porch light flashes on and off.

Lorraine: Oh, for God's sake.

Sal: Who's that, your mother?

Lorraine: I do love you, Sal.

Sal: Swell. This sure wasn't in the plan.

*LORRAINE removes the diamond
necklace and lets it fall into his hand.*

Lorraine: It's gorgeous.

Sal: Come on, what is this? Keep it.

Lorraine: Take the mink with you.

Sal: What am I going to do with a mink?

Lorraine: I can't keep them.

Sal: Lorraine, please, come with me. Be my wife.

Lorraine: If you have feelings for me—

Sal: What is this *feelings*? I'm over the moon for you.

Lorraine: Please don't ask again.

Sal: I don't leave for a month yet. Think about it some more. Things'll look different in a month.

Lorraine: No. It's better this way. Now.

Sal: This is that mother of yours talking.

Lorraine: How can I make you understand?

Sal: Well, I *don't* understand. Going without you makes no sense.

Lorraine: And that's why you need to go alone.

Sal: That's it, then? You're turning me down?

Lorraine: I cannot be a tower of strength for one more person in this life.

The back porch light flashes again.

Sal: Hey! Knock it off with that light! (*To Lorraine*) What the hell are you talking about? I love you. You love me. This is a problem?

Lorraine: You're afraid, Sal.

Sal: I'm not afraid a nothing.

Lorraine: I don't think you realize it.

Sal: What, you think I need you to hold my hand in order to go legit?

Lorraine: You're a good man, Sal.

Sal: I must be some kind a joke to you.

Lorraine: You just don't know it yet.

> *HARRIET enters from her yard in bathrobe and slippers.*

Harriet: Who's the imbecile flashing all the lights?

Sal: Aw, jeez, now this.

Lorraine: Harriet, everything's fine. Go home.

> *ROSEMARY comes out onto the porch.*

Rosemary: It's Al Capone, Harriet. I've got a gangster in my back yard.

Lorraine: Do you mind?

Harriet: Might as well send Tojo a personal invitation.

Rosemary: Lorraine, it's time to come inside.

Sal: Hey, a little privacy!

> *HARRIET regards the TAKIMOTO*
> *yard on the other side.*

Harriet: Thought there might be more trouble over at the Takimotos.

Rosemary: Time for all gangsters to go home, and for all good young ladies to come inside.

Lorraine: I am no longer young.

Sal: You want gangster, I can give you gangster.
Rosemary: And now he's threatening me.

Lorraine: *(To Rosemary)* Go to bed. I'll be in when I come in.

Rosemary: I'm waiting on your defiant sister to come home.

Harriet: Where is she?

Rosemary: I'm sure she's at that dance club for servicemen.

Sal: This the way you want to leave it, then?

Lorraine: Let me call you.

Sal: What for?

Lorraine: To say goodbye properly.

Rosemary: Two words—*drop dead*—and that job is done.

Sal: Why don't you go bury a bone?

Lorraine: Sal…not my mother.

Sal: (*To Rosemary*) Congratulations. You win. I lose.

Rosemary: Oh, have my prayers been answered?

Sal: (*To Lorraine*) Maybe one day you'll realize I wasn't looking for a pair of shoulders to do my heavy lifting.

> *SAL pulls Lorraine into a long
> and passionate kiss.*

Rosemary: What a revolting display.

Sal: Could a grown old with you, kiddo. Hairless, toothless, varicose. Was even looking forward to it.

Lorraine: Sal—

Sal: Be happy, you hear me? All the best.

> *SAL flees the yard before his emotions betray him. He has left the mink behind.*

Lorraine: What have I done? Sal…

> *ROSEMARY comes off the porch and picks up the mink.*

Rosemary: …treating a piece this way. Your father had a vault built off my dressing room in the old house for my furs. Diamonds, perfume, mink. I know what they can mean to a woman. I'm sick to think what you had to do to get it.

Lorraine: The same thing you did to get yours.

Rosemary: I ought to slap your face.

> *LORRAINE moves to in front of*
>
> *ROSEMARY—a challenge.*

11

When nothing happens,

LORRAINE grabs the mink and heads inside.

(*Beat*) Go home, Harriet. I'm going to sit here and wait for Linda.

ROSEMARY sits in a lawn chair.

Harriet: I'm not sleepy.

HARRIET pulls another lawn chair up and sits.

Nice night for February. Warm.

Rosemary: I've been thinking about Herbert.

Harriet: You think too much.

Rosemary: Thirteen years ago tomorrow.

Harriet: His bank closed…took him ten years to die…mustard gas…despicable Germans…my life stood still. I don't need to hear this litany again.

HARRIET gets up to leave.

Rosemary: Oh, sit down. You may be German, but at least you're *our* German, not the filthy Hun.

Harriet: Here we are fighting them again. France is licked. Russia's in trouble. They say there are Jap U-Boats off the coast of Santa Barbara.

Rosemary: Fear-mongering rumor.

Harriet: Mark my words; there'll be a Japanese armada under the Golden Gate before spring.

Rosemary: We're promised an *inevitable triumph.*

Harriet: Only if we can stop them at Chicago. If not, they'll be marching down Pennsylvania Avenue.

Rosemary: Harriet, please, I can't bear the thought.

Harriet: They're going to own the Pacific in very short order.

Rosemary: Who was minding the store?

Harriet: (*Beat*) Linda out with that Delores again?

Rosemary: That's an alliance we're going to have to nip in the bud. Keep your ear to the ground.

Harriet: Fast company.

Rosemary: Tramp.

Harriet: Linda's a good girl.

Rosemary: I'm losing control and I don't like it.

Harriet: *(Beat)* Natsuko should get out of California while she still has the chance.

Rosemary: Could you if your husband had been rousted out in the middle of the night and held without a word God knows where?

Harriet: Any day now they're going to close the border and she won't have a choice.

Rosemary: *Voluntary evacuation*...I couldn't do it.

Harriet: She's smart she'll start selling out before everybody else does.

Rosemary: When the universe turns against you, you do what you can to hang on.

Harriet: ...trouble with being a Jap.

Rosemary: What?

Harriet: Hard to blend in. You can't just hang on.

Rosemary: Poor Natsuko.

Lights fade.

Two

Scene*:*

Early morning. A month later.

At Rise:

SAL is discovered in shirt-sleeves, a telephone receiver held to his ear.

Sal: Lorraine?

> *LORRAINE is discovered wearing shipyard welder's clothes. She holds a telephone receiver to her ear.*

Lorraine: It's me.

Sal: Everything all right?

Lorraine: I'm fine, Sal. I'm on break. Two shifts in a row plus mandatory overtime. I didn't know when else I'd get the chance to reach you. Did I wake you?

Sal: Lorraine…the sound of your voice…you have no idea.

Lorraine: Today's the big day?

Sal: Tonight. I'll be ready maybe next week. Who can sleep? I've been working around the clock.

> *LORRAINEfeels pressured to hurry*
> *by those waiting in line to use the*
> *phone booth.*

Lorraine: Look, they're watching the clock and there's a line for this phone around the building. I'm sorry, Sal, I did not want to complicate this but I need to see you if you'd be willing to see me.

Sal: Where are you? I'll be right there.

Lorraine: I'm not punched out yet. I'm hoping they'll let me go at the end of this eight. Can I buy you lunch?

Sal: No, but you can let me buy you the swankiest lunch you ever had.

Lorraine: I would like to see you before you go.

Sal: Lorraine, sweetheart, I hope this means you've changed your mind.

Lorraine: (*To those waiting, off*) Knock it off! I'll be done when I'm done! (*Into the phone*) Sorry. What?

Sal: Sapphire Room at the Beaumont, say, one o'clock?

Lorraine: Yes. I…I think I can do that.

Sal: This has been the longest month of my life, no kiddin'.

Lorraine: Sal—

Sal: You have no idea how many times I've picked up the phone—

Lorraine: Sal—

Sal: The thought of leaving town without seeing you again was killin' me—

Lorriane: Sal, I need to ask you for an outrageous favor.

Sal: Anything! You got it. Whatever.

Lorraine: See you at the Beaumont at one.

LORRAINE exits.

Sal: Fair warning, doll, I don't intend to give up so easily this time. Lorraine? Lorraine...?

SAL realizes that the call has been terminated. He is both stunned and hopeful.

Lights Fade.

Three

Scene:

One o'clock in the afternoon.

The yard is crowded with household items that have been brought over from the Takimoto house.

At Rise:

ROSEMARY packs the items to be stored in her attic for the duration. This will be the core of the physical activity for everyone throughout the play.

In addition to a few cardboard boxes, which are at a premium, virtually everything becomes a vessel for storage—crates, tubs, barrels, pots, pillow cases, baskets, bags, satchels, bound bundles, etc.

Her attention is drawn to the sky. She goes to the porch for binoculars, spots and tracks a plane, consults identification cards, and records the sighting in a ledger.

LORRAINE enters in work clothes. She carries a lunch pail, a purse, and a shopping bag.

THEY regard each other warily.

Lorraine: Every Jap in the city is waiting for a bus.

LORRAINE gets the silent treatment.

I'm all in.

More cold shoulder.

Look, not today. I don't have time. Any mail?

Rosemary: Another overdue notice on the refrigerator.

Lorraine: I mailed the payment yesterday.

Rosemary: We shouldn't rely on the Post Office when the bill is already overdue.

Lorraine: And what's all this?

Rosemary: I'm packing a few things away for Natsuko.

Lorraine: I wish you wouldn't do that.

Rosemary: Seems to me you've forgotten that she treated you like one of her own when you were younger.

Lorraine: I'm too busy thinking about the jeopardy you keep putting us in. I'm exhausted. And I'm late.

LORRAINE heads inside.

ROSEMARY is desperate to stop her.

Rosemary: Where do you think you're going?

Lorraine: I'm meeting Sal for lunch.

Rosemary: When did that start up again?

Lorraine: Nothing's starting up again. He's doing me a favor.

Rosemary: I'm a disgrace.

Lorraine: And a broken record.

LORRAINE heads inside.

ROSEMARY has to stop her.

Rosemary: Where *were* you all night?

Lorraine: I worked Wilma's shift after I finished mine. Her son hurt himself. She had to leave.

Rosemary: She's making a career out of that.

Lorraine: They called mandatory overtime at the end of her shift.

Rosemary: It's not the first time I've had to put two and two together.

Lorraine: There was a line at the five and dime. Two and a half hours later it turned out to be for stockings. I should have stayed on the bus.

Rosemary: The cowards tried to burn Natsuko out last night.

Lorraine: Is she all right?

Rosemary: There's not an unbroken window in her house.

Lorraine: Was she hurt?

Rosemary: Spineless slugs.

Lorraine: (*Of Natsuko's things*) Exactly why we shouldn't be doing this.

Rosemary: I've barely made a dent in it.

> *The RADIO is heard from inside.*
> *Big band dance music.*

Rosemary: Linda, you turn that thing off! She didn't get in until the wee hours this morning.

LINDA comes to the screen door.

Linda: Did you say something?

Rosemary: Turn it off.

Linda: Gee-whiz.

LINDA goes to turn off the radio.

Rosemary: Don't gee-whiz-me. I want it quiet. And what are you doing home from school at this hour?

LINDA bounces out of the house.

Lorraine: Is Harriet's cab in her driveway?

Linda: And who's been in my room?

Rosemary: Do you see me trying to have a conversation with your sister?

Linda: Can't I have any privacy?

LORRAINE heads inside.

Rosemary: Lorraine, I'm not through with you.

Lorraine: Linda, will you go over and see if Harriet's there?

>*The TELEPHONE rings three short and one long inside.*

And that's probably Sal.

Linda : I'll get it.

Rosemary: I will get the phone.

>*All three try to get inside.*

Linda: I'm expecting a call.

Rosemary: I will answer the phone.

Lorraine: Sal probably thinks I've stood him up.

Rosemary: I said I will be the one to answer the telephone!

>*ROSEMARY has commandeered the door and exits inside.*

Lorraine: Why'd you stay out so late last night? Now she's on a tear.

Linda: Look whose talking.

Lorraine: I'm never going to get out of here.

Linda: Miss Mobster-Gun-Moll.

Lorraine: Wise up.

Linda: You stink.

Lorraine: I need you to go over and ask Harriet to give me a ride down to the Beaumont Hotel.

Linda: Nope.

Lorraine: Please.

Linda: Do you understand how much I hate it here?

Lorraine: Not my idea of Easy Street either, kiddo.

Linda: Sometimes I don't think you were ever seventeen.

Lorraine: I never had that luxury.

Linda: I'm quitting school.

Lorraine: Knock it off. Go see if Harriet's home.

Linda: I'm going to get a job.

Lorraine: Why, is that what Delores is doing?

Linda: Maybe.

Lorraine: You're not quitting school, Linda. I won't let you.

Linda: Try and stop me.

Lorraine: You want to talk about what it was like for me at your age? I was a little preoccupied with a spoiled brat for a sister, and a mother too debilitated with grief to be of any use whatsoever. So, no, I don't really know what seventeen looks like. You want to challenge me? Go ahead and try, Linda. Try to quit school. Now get over there and see if Harriet will give me a ride!

Linda: Do you know how much I hate you?

Lorraine: I've got a good idea. Tell her I'll pay the fare.

> *LINDA is ready to comply when*

> *ROSEMARY comes out of the house.*

Rosemary: So, we're not feeling well, I understand.

Linda: Oh, swell.

Rosemary: That was your Principal. She tells me you're in agony, (*to Lorraine*) her term, (*back to Linda*) with lady problems again.

Linda: (*Feigning cramps*) I am. I was trying to tell you.

Rosemary: Lorraine, do you think we can afford to get Miss Thing here to a doctor? This has gone on far too long.

Lorraine: Let's try the Castor oil first.

Linda: I'll be all right.

Rosemary: When a problem persists this way, we need to try everything.

Linda: I'm feeling better.

Rosemary: We don't need to see friends, or talk on the telephone if we're in too much agony to go to school.

Linda: I'm not sick, okay!

Rosemary: Then you march your deceitful self back to school this instant.

LORRAINE goes inside before

ROSEMARY can stop her.

Rosemary: Lorraine! (*To Linda*) Well, thank you very much. Now we're going to have Hail Columbia inside and out.

Linda: Well, gee whiz, what did I do?

Rosemary: She doesn't know yet that Natsuko is sleeping in her room.

Linda: Uh-oh.

Rosemary: And where is your bicycle?

Linda: In the driveway.

Rosemary: The driveway is no place for a bicycle. Use it and get back to school.

LINDA picks up the shopping bag.

Linda: What's this?

Rosemary: Stockings. Let me see that.

LINDA brings her the bag.

You have no idea how I've needed these.

*ROSEMARY pulls out a box and
examines the stockings*

Rosemary: Oh, rayon.

*ROSEMARY hands the items back
to Linda.*

It's silk or nothing for me. Your sister can *have* them. Go to school.

Linda: The chain keeps coming off my bicycle. I had to walk it practically all the way home.

Rosemary: Harriet will have to fix it.

*HARRIET enters from her yard,
carrying a girl's jacket.*

Harriet: Harriet will have to fix what?

Linda: The chain on my bike.

Harriet: Bring it over to my house and I'll have a look at it. Did you get the DC-3?

Rosemary: Of course.

Harriet: Figured it for Navy. Probably Moffet Field.

HARRIET surveys the yard.

Harriet: You've been out and around too, eh? Sidewalk sales everywhere. Not bad for Jap. Got a deal on a set of box wrenches and a car jack. Get a load of this—hydraulic.

> *HARRIET holds out the jacket to Linda.*

Got this for you. Think it'll fit. Try it on.

> *LINDA slips into the jacket.*

What are you doing out of school?

Rosemary: Same old story.

> *LINDA takes the jacket off.*

Harriet: Come on, hop in the cab. I'll drive you back to school.

Linda: I don't like the jacket.

Harriet: (*To Rosemary*) Cost me six bits.

> *LORRAINE charges out of the house.*

Lorraine: You want the bricks to start coming through our windows?

Rosemary: They tried to incinerate the woman.

Harriet: What's happened?

Linda: Mom took in Mrs. Takimoto.

Harriet: Lousy idea. Bad.

Rosemary: Don't you start with me, Harriet. Where were you last night when the commotion started?

Harriet: At the bowling alley praying for pinnage.

Rosemary: You can't tell me this entire neighborhood didn't hear it.

Harriet: I wasn't home, I tell you.

Lorraine: Exactly what I'm trying to head off.

Harriet: She hurt?

Rosemary: She'll not step foot back into that house alone, as far as I'm concerned.

Lorraine: Do you realize what this is going to make us?

Linda: Jap Rats!

Rosemary: You hush.

Linda: Well, that's what they call them.

Rosemary: I could not have raised either one of you without our neighbors.

Harriet: Well, now, that's true.

Lorraine: You raised no one. What happened last night?

Rosemary: (*Swallowing the barb*) I was lying in bed, worrying myself to death as to the whereabouts of daughter number one—

Linda: Lorraine didn't come home last night.

Lorraine: *(To Harriet)* I worked a double shift, plus overtime. *(To Linda)* Nice try.

Rosemary: I heard broken glass, milling about. I smelled fire.

Lorraine: Why didn't you call someone?

Rosemary: Thelma and Vi wouldn't get off the line.

Harriet: Old biddy hens. Viola Wainwright thinks she's the Queen of England. Well, P.S., she's not.

Linda: Mom scared them off by herself.

Lorraine: It just keeps getting worse.

Rosemary: *Jap Rat*, they yelled. *Stinking Jap Rat!* I told them I had called the police, and then I hurled one of their torches right back at them. They ran.

Harriet: Recognize anyone?

Rosemary: Too dark to see what with the blackout.

Lorraine: All right, I can still contain this. Does anyone know she's here?

Rosemary: Who can say?

Linda: Are we really Jap Rats?

Rosemary: Natsuko may be a Jap, but at least she's *our* Jap.

Harriet: Jap's a Jap nowadays.

Lorraine: Harriet, I've got to get down to the Waverly-Beaumont Hotel. I'm already late.

Harriet: I'd have to wash and wax the cab before I could pull her into the Beaumont!

Lorraine: Just slow down and kick me to the curb.

Harriet: That I can do.

Rosemary: Must you?

Lorraine: *(To Harriet)* I've got to change. *(To Rosemary)* You don't understand.

Rosemary: No, I certainly do not.

Lorraine: You've created another mess. I'll clean it up, but only if you stay out of the way.

> *NATSUKO TAKIMOTO comes out of the house. She has heard all.*

Rosemary: Natsuko.

Natsuko: Can someone tell me the time?

Rosemary: Did we wake you?

Natsuko: I couldn't sleep.

Harriet: Just after one o'clock.

> *A prisoner of her own home for the past month, NATSUKO steps off the porch sun-starved.*

Natsuko: The sun.

> *NATSUKO walks among her things in the yard.*

Natsuko: You've certainly been busy this morning.

34

Rosemary: We're going to store it all away for when you come back.

NATSUKO marks the presumptuous liberty.

Natsuko: Did you happen to get my purse?

Rosemary: Where would it have been?

Natsuko: Hanging on the back of the bedroom door.

Rosemary: Linda—no. Harriet.

HARRIET heads next door.

Harriet: I'll get it. I'll get it.

Natsuko: I would like to get a few personal items.

Harriet: What do you need?

Natsuko: (*Embarrassed*) Toothbrush, deodorant. …under things.

Harriet: Grab what I can.

Lorraine: Harriet, I'll only be a couple of minutes.

Harriet: Go. Go.

LORRAINE goes inside the house.

ROSEMARY follows.

Rosemary: *(Exiting)* Lorraine, you simply cannot start up with that wretched man again.

Linda: I don't mind sharing my room with Lorraine. Much. It'll be okay.

Natsuko: Your mother can be very determined.

Linda: Everything's different now, isn't it?

Natsuko: Very different.

Linda: I don't think of you as a Jap.

Natsuko: I don't think of you as a Jap Rat.

Linda: I have to get my bicycle. Harriet has to fix it.

LINDA retreats to the driveway.

NATSUKO'S attention is drawn to the sky. She uses the binoculars to make a sighting and records it in the ledger.

Lights fade.

Four

Early afternoon.

More Takimoto belongings have been brought over.

At Rise:

NATSUKO, now dressed, organizes her own belongings, gathering the linens piled here and there all together.

A RADIO sits on a porch table, along with a TELEPHONE. Big band music plays.

LINDA practices a new dance step.

ROSEMARY comes out and turns off the radio.

Rosemary: And what is my radio doing out here?

Linda: I'm trying to learn some new moves.

Rosemary: Learn to waltz and you'll be fit for any occasion.

Linda: I'd rather wear orthopedic shoes in a beauty contest.

ROSEMARY picks up the TELEPHONE.

Rosemary: You'll be wearing them just to stand upright if you don't stop using this telephone as your own personal instrument. I'm having Harriet switch us back to the short cord.

> *ROSEMARY takes the telephone back into the house.*

Linda: I can never do anything right.

Natsuko: I don't know what to say about that.

Linda: Don't you like us anymore?

Natsuko: It is no longer my place to like or dislike.

> *The TELEPHONE rings inside, three short, one long.*

> *LINDA goes on alert.*

Linda: (*Beat*) It's like you're invisible.

*NATSUKO cannot encourage
Linda's desire for intimacy.*

Natsuko: Invisible would be better.

Linda: Why didn't you and Mr. Takimoto leave when the borders were still open?

Natsuko: We never thought it would come to this.

Linda: Who knows what's going to happen anymore. *(Beat)* You used to fix my hair.

*Again, NATSUKO refuses to warm
to how things used to be.*

Natsuko: Yes.

Linda: With ribbons.

Natsuko: Yes.

*LINDA reaches out and touches
Natsuko.*

Linda: I loved your touch.

*NATSUKO regards Linda's
hand on her arm.*

LINDA retracts her hand.

Natsuko: (*Beat*) Yes.

> *ROSEMARY comes out of the house.*

Rosemary: Who is Moose Hollenbeck, Seaman, First Class?

Linda: Did he call?

Rosemary: He's on the phone.

> *Like a puppy to the chow, LINDA*
> *dashes inside.*

You are not leaving this house, young lady. You're sick, remember?

> (*To Natsuko*)

I believe we've just found out why she refused to go back to school.

Natsuko: Yes.

Rosemary: I've told her I don't want her going to those dance places. They're full of servicemen.

Natsuko: You have good daughters.

Rosemary: I can't help but think I've failed them. Herbert must be rolling in his grave.

Natsuko: I am no longer used to such conversation.

Rosemary: I thought Lorraine was going to be an only child. Herbert rallied there for almost a year. Linda took us by surprise.

Natsuko: Where once we enjoyed easy conversation, there is danger for me now of over-stepping myself at every turn.

Rosemary: Not with me.

Natsuko: You should be more cautious, Rosemary.

Rosemary: Nonsense. I've shared what was on my mind. Your turn now. Anything. Just say something, Natsuko. Go on. We'll be back to where we were in no time, you and I. *(Beat)* Do it!

Natsuko: *(With difficulty)* When Mary came to her father determined to marry a hukajin boy—a white boy—Yoshio was blind to everything but her defiance. He banished her. It broke my heart.

Rosemary: I remember. So hard on you. Torn.

Natsuko: Ordinarily we do not share such things.

Rosemary: These are not ordinary times.

Natsuko: No.

Rosemary: More.

Natsuko: I always had affection for Steven. It was not that we didn't like him. It was that he wasn't one of us.

Rosemary: What the world has come to—us, them.

Natsuko: Yoshio came around eventually. But for a time there was bitter silence.

Rosemary: Yes. *(Beat)* Oh, don't stop now. We're winning. Keep talking.

Natsuko: I admired Mary's determination. I said nothing. But I did not agree with Yoshio. He knew it. It remains an unhealed wound.

> *They warm to each other as once they*
> *must have done without care.*

Rosemary: Chicago. I always wondered, their moving so far away. Family was so important to you. And to Yoshio, never mind the differences.

Natsuko: The move spared her the shame she would have seen in her father's eye.

Rosemary: Have you heard from them? What's it like for your people in Chicago?

Natsuko: I have told her not to call. And to stop writing. The telephone is monitored. The mail is checked. Almost anything can cause an arrest. I miss her very much.

Emotion betrays NATSUKO's resolve.

I would like to meet my grandson.

ROSEMARY offers a warm embrace.

It is a comfort that they will not have to report like we do.

Rosemary: You should have gone to Chicago at Christmas. It was the perfect time.

Natsuko: Yoshio would not go. I will never willingly leave the home we built together. Where would he go if they release him?

Rosemary: To the racetrack, I suppose, like everyone else.

Natsuko: They are building camps.

Rosemary: In the meantime, you'll be lucky to be indoors. At best that's going to mean a horse stall. No telling what vermin they're infested with. Barbaric.

Natsuko: I try not to think about it.

Rosemary: I couldn't bear it.

Natsuko: Where is the farthest place you've ever been?

Rosemary: Greece, to see the antiquities, on our honeymoon. Lorraine was conceived there. We made the grand tour.

Natsuko: For me it was Monterey. Yoshio had been invited to address an organization interested in growing orchids. We took the train after breakfast and arrived before lunch, yet it felt like we had gone to the edge of the earth. I have never been anywhere, Rose. How could I leave on my own?

Rosemary: Have you considered not reporting?

Natsuko: We must show our loyalty by not complaining.

Rosemary: Bunk.

Natsuko: I do not have the defiance in me that my daughter had.

Rosemary: I'd like to see you fight this thing. What's the worst they could do, lock you up? Seems to me they're going to do that anyway?

Natsuko: It is better that I go.

Rosemary: I've done some checking. There are people who will help, the American Friends Service Committee. They can make an appeal. The American Civil Liberties—

Natsuko: No, Rosemary, no. You must stop! No more checking. No more asking questions that have no answers. No more this charade of neighborly backyard chat.

Rosemary: Natsuko, you don't seem able or willing to save yourself.

Natsuko: It would not be of any help. You will only make it worse by calling attention to me. And if attention is brought to me, it will make it that much worse for Yoshio. There has already been too much shame for one life. It is enough that he will know I did what was given me to do. That I did not run away.

Rosemary: Neighbors all these years, we're still a world apart.

Natsuko: Do you not see what I am?

Rosemary: You were wonderful to my girls when I was…less than able. That's what I remember.

Natsuko: Friendship means nothing anymore. You will still be living here after I am gone. Lorraine understands that. You do not.

Rosemary: I am not the woman I started out to be in this life. I'd like to do one thing that is not peevish and self-centered. Something good.

Natsuko: You cannot save me, Rose. You must stop trying.

HARRIET enters wheeling Linda's bike.

Harriet: Here we are good as new.

Rosemary: Why aren't you on the road with the meter running?

Harriet: That's the nice thing about being an independent. Set your own hours. I do a good morning business. Afternoons are slow. I'll head out later for the supper club crowd.

LINDA comes out of the house.

Linda: Harriet, Mrs. Wallace keeps cutting into my conversation, and someone's at the door!

Rosemary: I want you off that instrument, young lady.

Harriet: (*Of the bicycle*) Got the chain fixed for you.

Linda: She wants to know if you'll come over and look at her radiator.

Harriet: Tell Thelma I'll be there presently.

LINDA goes back inside.

You two stay put. I'll get the door.

Rosemary: Harriet, she's on the phone with a boy named Moose. Find out what you can.

HARRIET offers a thumbs-up and goes inside.

Rosemary: Honestly, the things I'm forced to do. Now, I've asked Lorraine to see if there's anyone down at the shipyard who would be interested in renting your house. I figure we'll lease it, manage it, and rent it furnished. It should certainly provide enough for taxes, and some extra, if we're lucky.

Again, NATSUKO must swallow Rosemary's presumptuous liberties.

Natsuko: What's the point? They have frozen all the bank accounts.

Rosemary: I can send money to you every month.

LINDA bounds out of the house.

Linda: Mom, it's Costello's! They've come for the refrigerator!

Rosemary: They're what?

Linda: Said we owed them money, and they're going to repossess it.

Suddenly it's a farce.

LINDA rushes in.

HARRIET rushes out.

Harriet: Thirty-six dollars or they're taking it.

HARRIET searches the Takimoto goods for weaponry.

Rosemary: I've told Lorraine repeatedly, go down and pay your bills in person.

Harriet: Did the same thing to Blanche. Came and took her automatic washer. Wouldn't give her the chance to make amends.

Rosemary: I don't have thirty-six dollars.

HARRIET has found a hammer

and a rolling pin.

Harriet: Want me to handle it?

Rosemary: No! Put those down.

LINDA comes out again, irate.

Linda: Well, thanks, everybody, he just hung up!

LINDA goes back inside.

Harriet: They won't know what hit them!

HARRIET heads inside with the hammer and the rolling pin.

Rosemary: She'll kill them.

Natsuko: Take *my* refrigerator. I won't need it.

Rosemary: Stay out here. I don't want anyone to see you.

ROSEMARY heads inside.

NATSUKO retreats to packing her own belongings.

LORRAINE and SAL enter from around the side of the house.

SAL flashes a wad of bills.

Sal: Let me pay them the thirty-six dollars.

Lorraine: Put that away. This is not your problem.

Sal: Let me talk to them.

Lorraine: No interference. Promise me.

Sal: I promise. I promise.

Lorraine: Natsuko, he is not to come inside the house.

Sal: Let me call my father—this problem goes away (*snapping his fingers*) like that.

Lorraine: You're through with that, remember?

Sal: Go. I'm a statue.

LORRAINE goes inside.

SAL regards Natsuko and marks her confusion.

You got to watch this outfit. They been selling the same merchandise over and over. Just about get it paid off, they figure out a way to come and take it. I told Lorraine when she put money down that these were not class people. I could have gotten her a refrigerator. And below cost yet. No! The mother, of course. (*Beat*) So, you're the Jap neighbor, eh?

SAL offers his hand.

Salvatore Pasquaneri.

Awkwardly, NATSUKO gives Sal her hand.

Sal: Everybody calls me Sal.

Natsuko: Mrs. Yoshio Takimoto.

Sal: Right. See how I knew that?

Natsuko: You know me…?

Sal: You got the daughter living back east, Chicago, right?

Natsuko: (*Alarmed*) How do you know that?

Sal: I'm headed there myself. Tonight, as a matter of fact. Business. Bought into a plant. Dehydrated foods. Going to be big. Very big.

Natsuko: What does that have to do with my daughter?

Sal: There is no end to where this business can go. Dehydrated foods are going to change the way the world sits down to dinner. Bigger than big. Huge.

Natsuko: What is the point of this?

Sal: Hard day, come home, open a bag, hydrate, boil, eat. Turkey, roast beef, leg a lamb, whatever. You're hearing it now. Bigger than huge.

Natsuko: Dehydrated food.

Sal: I'm starting with these little tins, you know? Rations. For the soldiers over seas. Already lined up a government contract. Lend Lease. Best thing ever happened to business since the cash register. Gigantic!

Natsuko: My daughter does not know you.

Sal: Can't get into this fight. Might as well feed those who can, right? Army, Navy, Marine Corps. No! Bad back. Football, you know. This way at least, I'm pulling my weight.

Natsuko: Do you work for the government?

Sal: No. I am a legitimate businessman. Look how nice you are. These people talking about *yellow peril*, what is that?

Natsuko: Fear.

Sal: Lorraine tells me you been taking a real beating.

Natsuko: I have not complained.

Sal: She tells me that too.

> *SAL indicates first Harriet's yard then the Takimoto's yard.*

Sal: Which side are you on, over here? There?

Natsuko: There. My husband built it.

> *SAL surveys the Takimoto yard.*

Sal: Yeah, regular vigilante stuff. They tried to burn you out?

Natsuko: I have made no complaint.

Sal: And you're shipping out any day now?

Natsuko: I must report for relocation tomorrow.

Sal: No wonder Lorraine's got a fire lit under her.

Natsuko: No one knows that. I don't know why I told *you*.

Sal: People tell me things. I listen. It's how I know stuff.

Natsuko: I would prefer not to say anything else.

Sal: This is not a good business.

Natsuko: There is nothing to be done.

Sal: And your husband. Lorraine tells me they've got him in stir somewhere.

Natsuko: Stir?

Sal: Guest of good ole Uncle Sam.

Natsuko: They came for him in the middle of the night. I do not know where they are holding him.

Sal: Stinks.

Natsuko: I received a letter in his hand. He wrote that he is well, and that I was not to be afraid.

Sal: No, this is a lousy business.

Natsuko: It was the first time he had ever written to me in English.

Sal: These are not class people.

Natsuko: He must have been forced to write in English. He would not have done so otherwise.

Sal: What did he do to get pinched?

Natsuko: Pinched?

Sal: Arrested.

Natsuko: He received a tribute from a Japanese trade organization, a wooden bowl honoring his many years in the nursery business. His picture was in the newspaper. They had it with them when they came to get him.

Sal: G-men. Thugs.

Natsuko: Our nursery was next to the power plant. They said the power plant was in danger. Our nursery was there before the power plant was built.

Sal: I'm glad I can help out.

Natsuko: I am not asking for help.

Sal: Not to worry. Lorraine asked me. I would do anything for her.

Natsuko: What is it you intend to do?

Sal: She didn't tell you?

Natsuko: No.

Sal: So you don't know what the shot is?

Natsuko: I know nothing about shots.

Sal: You're coming with me to Chicago. Tonight.

Natsuko: Chicago?

Sal: It's all arranged.

Natsuko: How could I go to Chicago?

Sal: They've closed the border on you people. We'll hop over it. Who's to know?

Natsuko: I cannot leave my husband.

Sal: Your husband has been taken from you. Don't you have family in Chicago?

Natsuko: My daughter. My grandson.

Sal: So what's the problem?

Natsuko: I would be a criminal.

Sal: Not the worst thing in the world.

Natsuko: It would not be good for my husband.

Sal: What are they going to do, lock him up?

Natsuko: But the treatment he might receive.

Sal: Has nothing to do with you. They're gonna treat him the way they're gonna treat him.

Natsuko: I cannot bear the thought.

Sal: I can deliver you to your daughter in Chicago. I would like to do that. For Lorraine.

Natsuko: Chicago…

> *LINDA rushes on, followed by*
>
> *ROSEMARY and LORRAINE.*

Linda: Sal! You know your Packard out front?

Sal: *(On alert)* What about it?

Lorraine: There's been an accident.

Sal: Accident?

Natsuko: *(To Lorraine)* You have gone too far.

> *HARRIET enters and throws down
> the hammer and the rolling pin.*

Harriet: Sorry about that.

Lorraine: Sal, you'd better come out front.

Sal: Just tell me.

Linda: They dropped the refrigerator on the hood of your car.

Lorraine: The men from Costello's were trying to lift it onto the truck.

SAL runs out toward the front yard.

Sal: That's my father's Packard. It's a showpiece.

LORRAINE, LINDA, and HARRIET follow him out.

Rosemary: Natsuko, what is it?

Natsuko: Who do you people think you are? *(Beat)* Chicago…

Lights Fade.

Five

Scene:

*A short while later. Yet more items have
been brought over from next door.*

At Rise:

LINDA is on the porch tuning the radio.

*SAL hobbles out of the house in shirt sleeves…and a
lot of pain. He has injured his back moving the
Takimoto refrigerator over from next door.*

Sal: Holy mackerel, that refrigerator weighed more
than a Buick.

Linda: Shouldn't have moved it yourself.

Sal: You're telling me. Think I broke my back.

Linda: Harriet's good at backs. Want me to get her?

Sal: Tell you what, let's wait on that.

Linda: She can set bones, stop bleeding, sew up wounds, give injections.

Sal: That's swell. Think I'll be all right.

Linda: She was an ambulance driver in the last war.

Sal: Impressive.

Linda: She was with an aero squadron.

Sal: I gotta sit down.

> *SAL settles into a yard chair.*

Linda: She saw a mechanic get his hand chopped off in a propeller. Blood everywhere.

Sal: You enjoyed that?

Linda: Another time, she had wounded soldiers in the back and something went wrong and she had to crawl under the ambulance and fix it, and these German soldiers came up...

Sal: *(Intrigued now)* Yeah...and?

Linda: I forget, but anyway she got the ambulance going again, so I'm sure she can fix your car.

Sal: You're killin' me.

Linda: She owns a cab. Does all her own repairs.

Sal: Swell. Where's your sister?

Linda: Who cares?

Sal: I'm never gonna get out of here.

Linda: Why *did* you move Mrs. Takimoto's refrigerator by yourself? You don't seem like…

Sal: Like what?

Linda: That type of man.

Sal: Come again?

Linda: It's not going to work.

Sal: This some kind of code?

Linda: You're trying to weasel your way into my mother's good graces.

SAL stretches the pain out of his back.

Sal: Yeah, well, it was a bum idea.

Linda: Everyone knows about your family.

61

Sal: And here we go down that road.

Linda: Who your father is. Your brothers.

Sal: You are some piece a work, sister.

Linda: You're notorious.

Sal: I am a legitimate businessman.

Linda: What kind of business?

Sal: Dehydrated foods.

Linda: My friend Delores says you're a loan shark.

Sal: Your friend Delores wise?

Linda: And not a very good one.

Sal: Tell you what, why don't we try a little silence.

Linda: You couldn't collect the vig.

Sal: The *vigorish!* Hello language. Nomenclature even.

Linda: Ended up an embarrassment to your family.

Sal: The mother, okay. Now the sister. Any chance Lorraine was adopted?

Linda: A laughing stock, as a matter of fact.

Sal: Second thought…were you?

Linda: Delores's father is a Longshoreman.

Sal: So that's it, Delores holds a grudge, eh? Tough childhood? Forced to toe a stern line?

Linda: Word on the street is your family can't get you out of town fast enough.

Sal: You got some mouth on you, little girl.

Linda: I am not a little girl!

Sal: No, I can see that. It would be a mistake to underestimate you, wouldn't it?

Linda: Yes.

Sal: *(Beat)* I had my way we'd end up related.

Linda: I had my way we'd end up something else.

Sal: Whoa, slow down, sister. You are way out of line.

Linda: So straighten me out.

Sal: You want the truth?

Linda: What I want I can't say out loud. I wasn't raised that way.

Sal: You and Delores, I'll bet, eh? Coupla fast ladies?

Linda: You're not going to tellthe truth, are you?

Sal: Yeah, I had money on the street for awhile. Didn't work out.

Linda: So, it's true then.

Sal: You nailed it, kiddo. Must be a real clown on the street if it's common knowledge to the likes of you and Delores. Longshoremen I could understand.

Linda: I think Lorraine was a bad influence. She ruined you.

Sal: She saved my life. I'd do anything for her.

Linda: That include saying goodbye?

Sal: If that's what she wants.

Linda: That's where Lorraine and I are completely different. She doesn't know what she wants.

Sal: Your sister is a very smart woman.

Linda: How did you meet her?

Sal: This guy owed me money. And now it's double the original note. So I go to where he works. I see him and already he starts to run. We do the chase. I corner him. Rough him up. People are standing around. Why doesn't someone step in? No. I've got to do this. So I take this length of pipe. He's crying now. He's begging me. He's dog meat. He's a bum. Call me a schmuck…I cannot stand to see a man cry in public that way.

Linda: *(With a surprising thirst for blood)* You break some bones?

SAL shakes his head.

LINDA is disappointed.

So, it *is* true then.

Sal: I dropped the pipe and walked away.

Linda: What a shame.

Sal: Now my hand starts throbbing and swelling up. I go over to this canteen truck and bury my hand in all the shaved ice on the side. Then over my shoulder reaches this shapely length of arm, going for the pimiento-cheese on the top shelf. Only she can't reach so good. I get the sandwich, turn around…haven't had eyes for anyone since.

Linda: Lorraine.

> LORRAINE is discovered in work clothes. She carries a sandwich wrapped in butcher paper.

Sal: Beautiful.

Lorraine: Thanks.

Sal: Don't mention it.

Lorraine: Looks like you've hurt your hand.

Sal: Funny…doesn't hurt anymore.

Lorraine: I'd get that looked at.

Sal: Any suggestions?

Lorraine: If you don't have a doctor, I'd go to a hospital.

Sal: No saw-bones for me.

Lorraine: May I look at it.

> *SAL holds up his hand.*

LORRAINE cradles it gently.

Sal: Your touch could be a cure for cancer.

Lorraine: It's starting to swell.

Sal: Or the cause of some serious heartache.

Lorraine: Am I going to have to worry about you?

Sal: It's a start.

Lorraine: You don't work here.

Sal: I'm thinking of applying.

Lorraine: There's a First Aide Department. Mostly aspirin and mercurochrome.

Sal: I would follow you anywhere.

Lorraine: It's only for employees.

Sal: What time do you punch out?

Lorraine: Three o'clock.

Sal: I'll be right outside that gate.

Lorraine: You need to go to a hospital.

Sal: So, I'll go at three o'clock.

Lorraine: It could be broken.

Sal: Small price to pay.

Lorraine: What will you do until then?

Sal: Stand right outside that gate.

Lorraine: I'm starting to worry about you.

Sal: Then you won't forget me.

Lorraine: I won't forget you.

Sal: My lucky day.

Lorraine: I've got to go back in.

Sal: I've got to go stand outside that gate.

Lorraine: I can see it from my place on the line.

Sal: Then I'll be on my best behavior.

Lorraine: Lorraine.

Sal: Sal.

Lorraine: It's supposed to rain.

Sal: Sounds like I'm gonna get wet.

Lorraine: I've got to go in.

Sal: I'm going to watch you walk away until I can't see you anymore.

Lorraine: Then I'll have to be on my best behavior.

Sal: Already we're good for each other.

Lorraine: See you at three.

Sal: If I'm not there, check the morgue, because it could only mean that I'm dead.

Lorraine: Don't get yourself killed.

Sal: Whatever you say.

     LORRAINE reluctantly exits.

Linda: Did you wait outside the gate until three?

Sal: I did.

Linda: You in love with her?

Sal: That you have to ask makes me think you're not as smart as *you* think you are.

Linda: Lorraine's a fool.

Sal: Only a fool would say so.

Linda: She should go with you.

Sal: No argument from me.

Linda: I'd go to Chicago in a heart beat.

Sal: Would you now.

Linda: I'd do anything to get out of here.

Sal: In kind of a hurry, aren't you?

Linda: If the world is coming to an end, I don't want to spend another minute being ordinary.

Sal: This war isn't going to last forever.

Linda: Maybe not, but it sure looks like we're going to lose it.

Sal: Says who, Delores?

Linda: Headlines, news reels, radio.

LINDA starts moving to the dance music.

I'm a better dancer than Lorraine.

Sal: Hard to believe.

Linda: I am though.

Sal: When she's on the floor, other dames tend to sit down.

Linda: This is a jitterbug.

Sal: We prefer it smooth and slow.

Linda: You hep to the jive?

Sal: How bad you want to find out?

> *LINDA turns up the volume.*

> *SAL is an excellent dancer and puts Linda through some moves that surprise her—jumping, turning, through the legs.*

> *ROSEMARY, LORRAINE, and NATSUKO enter from next door with several pieces of luggage.*

Rosemary: What in the world?

> *SAL puts Linda through an over-the-shoulder move that throws his back out. He is in*

agony and cannot stand up.

Sal: Holy mackerel!

Rosemary: Not in my own back yard.

SAL is down on all fours.

Sal: Holy Christmas!

Linda: He moved Mrs. Takimoto's refrigerator by himself.

Sal: Holy Jeez!

ROSEMARY turns the radio off.

Rosemary: You get in that house, young lady.

LORRAINE tries to help SAL.

Lorraine: Can you sit down?

Rosemary: What a crude spectacle.

SAL is on his belly on the ground.

Sal: I'm in agony here!

Lorraine: Linda, go get Harriet.

Sal: No! Do not get Harriet!

Rosemary: I knew the minute he showed up there was going to be trouble.

> *ROSEMARY has Linda by the ear lobe and pulls her into the house.*

March, young lady. There are some things we're not going to have around here.

Linda: Mom. Gee whiz. Ow!

> *NATSUKO looks on, helpless.*

Lorraine: Natsuko, go get Harriet.

Sal: No! Do not get Harriet! No!

> *HARRIET comes around the house, sets her toolbox down, and wipes her hands with a rag.*

Harriet: Intake on the carburetor is all mashed up, and the radiator is ruptured. I'm going to need some parts. What's wrong with beefcake there?

Lorraine: Threw his back out.

Harriet *(Rolling up her sleeves)* Can't have that.

HARRIET approaches SAL.

I can get her running, but it's going to take a body-man to pound out that hood.

Sal: Lorraine.

Harriet: Salvage yard might have what we need.

> *HARRIET grabs Sal by the collar*
> *and brings him to a sitting position.*

Sal: Lorraine.

Harriet: Hold your breath. You won't feel a thing.

Sal: What are you going to do?

> *Kneeling behind Sal, HARRIET*
> *engages a half Nelson and twists*
> *him savagely from side to side.*

Holy Christmas! Mother a God!

> *HARRIET lays him out flat.*

Don't you ever speak to me again, Lorraine!

Harriet: And now for the secret weapon.

> *HARRIET straddles his middle*

and grabs Sal by the belt.

Sal: No, no, no, no! Not the belt! Not the belt!

> *HARRIET yanks him into the air and bounces him several times then lays him down again.*

Harriet: Better?

Sal: What are you, sadistic?

> *HARRIET flips Sal onto his belly.*

Harriet: Hold on.

Sal: Uncle! Uncle!

> *HARRIET grasps Sal under the chin and bends his head back toward his feet three times then dismounts, swatting his behind to signal that she's done.*

Harriet: That should do it. Good as new.

Sal: They ought to put you on the front line.

Harriet: I got one more.

> *SAL jumps to his feet.*

Sal: I'm fine! Fine! No kidding. See?

Harriet: Works like a charm.

Sal: Lorraine, front yard, now!

SAL heads out, muttering.

Ought to have my head examined, getting mixed up with a family full a women.

LORRAINE follows out.

Harriet: Hey, I get the parts, I can fix it! *(To Natsuko)* Never got my hands on a Packard before.

HARRIET notes all the luggage.

Sure don't travel light, do you?

Natsuko: That is Rosemary's doing.

Harriet: Nothing halfway about that broad.

Natsuko: Lorraine has become the same way.

Harriet: Forget what they *say*, they're very much attached.

Natsuko: She has found her strength.

Harriet: Not sure anymore which one's the mother, which the daughter.

Natsuko: I cannot say no to either one of them.

Harriet: You're not going to go, are you?

Natsuko: I must prove my loyalty by reporting like everyone else.

Harriet: Thought so.

Natsuko: I will not run away.

Harriet: When are you going to tell them?

Natsuko: They refuse to listen.

Harriet: No, no, they listen. They don't always hear.

Natsuko: I would like to stay in my own home until the last moment.

Harriet: (*Of the luggage*) What's the allotment, one bag a piece?

Natsuko: Only what you can carry.

Harriet: How do you pack for the rest of your life?

Natsuko: Assume the worst. (*Of her household belongings*) And stop caring about *things*.

Harriet: You been over to the Tanforan Race Track?

Natsuko: No.

Harriet: Barbed wire. Guard towers.

Natsuko: They say it is for our own protection.

Harriet: The guns aren't pointed *out*, Natsuko.

Natsuko: You think I am foolish.

Harriet: Nope. Selfish.

Natsuko: Because I wish to be left alone?

Harriet: Because these gals are more important to me than blood-relatives. You've turned them into Jap Rats.

Natsuko: I tried to prevent that.

Harriet: Chicago, the camps…damage is done.

Natsuko: Yes.

Harriet: Still, I'm voting for Chicago.

Natsuko: You too?

Harriet: It'd get you out of here today. And that would be sooner than tomorrow.

Natsuko: Do you know what it turns you into knowing you are getting your neighbor dirty simply by accepting kindness?

Harriet: Spare me that song and dance. My name was Schmidt during the last war.

Natsuko: Yes. Of course.

Harriet: You remember.

Natsuko: I had forgotten.

Harriet: Our turn for the threats, rocks through the windows at night, hooligans.

Natsuko: Yes.

Harriet: I proved *my* loyalty by driving an ambulance in France. It's how I met my fly-boy. (*Beat*) Married him. Took his name. Delivered myself from the persecution.

Natsuko: Your good fortune.

Harriet: Good fortune had no part of it. I knew what had to be done. I did it.

Natsuko: You didn't love him?

Harriet: Did you love Yoshio when you married him?

Natsuko: I did not know him. He wrote to me. I came.

Harriet: We're not so different.

Natsuko: If only it was as easy as changing one's name.

Harriet: *(Beat)* He ended up the most exciting individual I'd ever known, man or woman. I knew *that* would never come again. Had the sense not to look for it.

Natsuko: I have built my life around Yoshio.

Natsuko: Here I am the *bachelor-woman* at the end of the street…fixes things for other people.

Natsuko: I do not expect him to survive the war.

Harriet: No word?

Natsuko: Just the one letter.

Harriet: *(Beat)* I *was* luckier than you.

Natsuko: Shikata ga ni. There is nothing to be done.

Harriet: *(Sotto voce)* Gott in Himmel.

> *They hear a plane.*

> *HARRIET makes the sighting.*

Harriet: Lockheed Lodestar.

> *HARRIET hands the binoculars*
> *to Natsuko.*

Two twelve hundred horsepower engines, nine cylinders each. She'll do two hundred fifty miles an hour easy. Sassy thing's going to help win this war.

> *NATSUKÒ watches the plane.*

> *HARRIET records the sighting.*

Lights Fade.

Six

Scene:

A short while later. The yard is at its fullest with Takimoto belongings— it just won't end. The packing has grown more urgent. Best not to be discovered aiding and abetting the enemy.

NATSUKO'S luggage remains from the previous scene.

At Rise:

LORRAINE throws things into her basket or tub with little care, while

NATSUKO cherishes each item before packing it away in hers.

Natsuko: The windows would have to be fixed. The front needs paint—the profanity.

Lorraine: Harriet's already started.

Natsuko: Where is the child's father?

Lorraine: He was on the Arizona.

Natsuko: *(Beat)* She knows it is a Japanese home?

Lorraine: She has no choice. There's a housing shortage.

Natsuko: Not anymore.

Lorraine: I told her about you.

Natsuko: She is a friend of yours?

Lorraine: I've never had time for friends. We work together. I know her. Her name is Wilma.

Natsuko: Thank you for the pretense of asking. We both know it is I who has no choice.

Lorraine: She could pay enough to cover the taxes.

Natsuko: The yard would be nice for a child.

Lorraine: I'll tell her she can move in.

Natsuko: The government would only confiscate it the way they did the nursery.

ROSEMARY comes out of the house.

Rosemary: I have your daughter on the line.

Natsuko: Mary? Called here?

Rosemary: I placed the call.

Natsuko: You have made a serious mistake.

Rosemary: She would like to speak with you.

    NATSUKO hesitates.

And it is long distance, person-to-person.

    NATSUKO hurries inside.

Watch what you say. Remember Thelma and Vi.

Lorraine: Have you lost your mind completely?

Rosemary: She needed a little push.

Lorraine: Well don't just stand there, get a box and fill it. Natsuko's pulling a slow-down. I've just rented the house.

    ROSEMARY packs a box but cannot match Lorraine's dispatch.

Rosemary: I knew you'd handle that. I just knew.

HARRIET comes out for more packed items.

Harriet: You know who she's talking to in there?

Rosemary: We certainly do.

Lorraine: Don't waste your breath, Harriet. She's a loose cannon.

Harriet: No telling who's listening in on that line.

Rosemary: They'll need a ride, what with *his* car in the condition it's in.

Harriet: I'm way ahead of you.

Lorraine: *His* name is Sal.

Rosemary: One good deed and you expected my heart would melt?

Lorraine: The man is going out of his way to help.

Rosemary: *(Disgusted)* Throwing a young girl around in such a vulgar manner.

HARRIET gathers several packed items.

Harriet: You want all these in the attic?

Rosemary: If there's room.

Harriet: I'll make room.

HARRIET takes a load into the house.

Lorraine: It wouldn't kill you to show a little appreciation for the risk he's taking.

Rosemary: Your father's probably rolling in his grave.

Lorraine: According to you he's done nothing but spin like a top ever since we put him in the ground.

Rosemary: Show some respect! I'm grateful he's not here to witness my disgrace.

Lorraine: I'm sure he knows.

Rosemary: Well, thank you very much. I never thought I'd end my days so...*common.*

Lorraine: You're not the only woman who's had to step down in life. You just think you are.

Rosemary: If I faltered it was because your sister was a baby. I had my hands full.

Lorraine: It was my hands that were full, Mother. You were too busy wringing yours.

Rosemary: I beg your pardon?

Lorraine: I took the responsibility. You took to your bed.

Rosemary: I never thought I'd see the day when I'd have to take in other people's laundry.

Lorraine: You did no one's laundry.

Rosemary: I was not bred to wash other people's clothes. It was they who were supposed to wash mine.

Lorraine: And you never once did your own laundry. I was responsible for that too.

Rosemary: I'm not blind to the fact that you've been burdened with a great deal. I don't have your fortitude, Lorraine. If I could just do this one unselfish thing…perhaps I could find my way back.

Lorraine: Why now? Why this?

Rosemary: I've no idea. It chose me.

LORRAINE resumes packing.

Lorraine: Let's get this stuff out of sight.

ROSEMARY assumes Lorraine's

vigor with the packing.

Rosemary: No matter what we've got to pave the way for your sister. She is the repository of all my hopes for the future. I cannot fail her too.

Lorraine: Linda. Always Linda.

LINDA runs on from out front.

Linda: Tow truck! Tow truck!

Rosemary: You were instructed to stay in your room, young lady. Where have you been?

Linda: Out front with Sal.

Rosemary: I do not want you near that man. Now you go back up to your room until I say you can come out. Lock the door.

Linda: Gee whiz!

LINDA goes inside as

SAL enters from out front.

Sal: My father is going to blow sky high he sees his Packard on the back of that truck.

Lorraine: Harriet is going to drive you.

Sal: Do we have a decision? The clock is ticking, people.

Rosemary: *(With Herculean effort)* Mr. Pasquaneri.

Sal: Sal. Just call me Sal.

Rosemary: Yes, well, Sal, I feel you are doing uh…what you're doing for Natsuko, Mrs. Takimoto, is, well, very—

Sal: I'm doing it for Lorraine.

Rosemary: Still, it is appreciated.

Sal: Let me understand something. You trying to be nice to me?

Rosemary: Actually, I'm trying not to vomit.

Sal: You're welcome.

    ROSEMARY flees inside.

Like seeing *her* on the run for a change.

Lorraine: That was for my benefit.

Sal: At least she tried.

Lorraine: She's not a bad woman. Life just didn't follow the same rules she did.

Sal: And you've got your work cut out for you with that Linda, no kiddin'.

Lorraine: I'm not sure there's anything more I can do for her.

Sal: I mean no disrespect here, but watch your back.

Lorraine: She sounding off again?

Sal: She may be your sister—I don't think she's your friend.

Lorraine: I've had to be the parent.

Sal: And I've said enough.

Lorraine: Whatever you see in them I'm sure is very much a part of me. They're my family.

Sal: Now who you sounding like?

Lorraine: You're a good man, Sal.

Sal: How can you be so sure?

> *LORRAINE places her hand*
> *over Sal's heart.*

90

Lorraine: This part of you right here. I'm surprised you don't see it.

Sal: I wish you knew what was in there.

Lorraine: It's a good heart.

Sal: The nearness of you. Your touch. It's racing.

Lorraine: I can feel it.

Sal: You own it. Belongs to you.

Lorraine: This may never come again.

Sal: You really going to let me walk away?

Lorraine: I've tried so hard to do the right thing.

    THEY kiss.

Sal: Come with me, Lorraine. Be my wife.

Lorraine: Mrs. Salvatore Pasquaneri.

Sal: My name never sounded so good.

Lorraine: I'm not sure, Sal.

Sal: Who's sure? Everything's a crap shoot. Take the leap.

Lorraine: I want to...

Sal: Then get out of your own way.

Lorraine: This is crazy.

Sal: A mother who's ashamed of you...a sister who hates you...and *this* is crazy?

Lorraine: We don't choose our families. We accept them.

Sal: Which is why I'm going to love them for you, kiddo. And take care of them. And protect them. Whether they want us to or not.

Lorraine: One last time, Sal. Let me hear it again.

> *Again, they embrace.*

Sal: Marry me, Lorraine. Be my wife.

Lorraine: Yes. Yes. Yes.

> *THEY kiss.*

Sal: How can we go wrong?

Lorraine: I'd better put something into a suitcase.

Sal: I'm gonna buy you everything you ever wanted. Head to toe. New beginning.

Lorraine: I don't want *things*, Sal. I want a life.

Sal: Mine feels like it's just beginning.

Lorraine: I'm going to trust that.

Sal: Gentlemen, start your engines.

One last kiss.

LORRAINE hurries inside.

It's a brand new day for SAL.

Lights Fade.

Seven

Late afternoon-early evening.

Natsuko's luggage is gone. Most of the household items have been cleared. Several boxes, bundles, parcels, etc., remain.

At Rise:

ROSEMARY, HARRIET, and LINDA pack the last of the belongings.

Rosemary: We never had a problem with the old icebox. Suddenly everybody's got to have new refrigerators.

> *SAL comes out of the house*
> *favoring his back. He loads up*
> *for another haul to the attic.*

Harriet: Nothing says that wretched Depression is over better than a new refrigerator, an automatic washer, or that new car in the driveway.

Rosemary: Then it's: *Did we make the payment? Is it supposed to run like that every minute of the day? Ice cubes!* What's next?

Sal: Dehydration! Meat, vegetable, dessert. What could be better?

Rosemary: Real food.

Sal: It's what's coming after this war. Count on it.

Linda: You could freeze them!

Sal: Trouble with frozen dinners is you have to keep them frozen.

Linda: Just an idea.

Sal: Refrigeration would kill you. You'd have to ship them frozen.

Harriet: Not impossible.

Rosemary: Dehydration befits the desert not the dinner table.

Sal: You'd have to store them frozen. Sell them frozen.

Linda: You mean like ice cream?

> *HARRIET and LINDA take packed
> items inside.*

Sal: *(Beat)* 'Course, no need to reconstitute with frozen.

> *ROSEMARY restores the yard to its
> former order—better even.*

Rosemary: When's the last time you ate a boiled meal?

Sal: Come again?

Rosemary: The baby's bottle, the three minute egg, the potato before it's mashed—a boiled meal is for those who cannot chew their food.

Sal: Uncle Sam does not agree with you. The G.I. in every theater of this war is sustained by dehydrated food.

Rosemary: You're suggesting we adopt the diet of a battlefield?

Sal: You're killin' me here, Mrs.

Rosemary: Now, *there's* an idea.

Sal: When you look at me, what do you see?

Rosemary: A well-cut suit.

Sal: Thanks. Havana. My cousin knows a guy who knows a guy.

Rosemary: My husband's tailor came to him. He never had to leave the country to dress well.

Sal: You see me all wrong.

Rosemary: I cannot see you for dust, and there it is.

Sal: Any chance you might come around on that?

Rosemary: Only if dementia were to set in.

Sal: You got a sharp mouth.

Rosemary: A woman alone, without resources, in a man's world, has to cultivate what strength she can.

Sal: Watch out you don't bite yourself.

Rosemary: I'm not wrong about you.

Sal: People change. Sometimes out of the blue.

Rosemary: Can that really be change...or just another failed attempt?

Sal: I could respect you because I love your daughter.

Rosemary: You are so far beneath my daughter as to barely be visible with the naked eye.

Sal: She says different.

Rosemary: You were the first man to bestow the kind of attention on her you have. She's not had an easy time of it. Lorraine will do the right thing.

Sal: Who's to say what's right?

Rosemary: She is a good girl on whom her sister and I depend.

Sal: She's a woman.

Rosemary: I would rather go to my grave than to see her ruin herself on the likes of you.

Sal: Lady, all I can say is...*prepare* yourself.

> *NATSUKO comes out of the house*
> *with one suitcase. She wears a coat*
> *and hat, and carries a purse.*

Natsuko: I am ready.

Rosemary: You're going?

Natsuko: Yes.

Sal: Swell! No kiddin'.

Rosemary: I couldn't bear to see you locked away like a common criminal.

Natsuko: You prefer to see me run away like one?

Rosemary: This evacuation is only on the west coast. You'll be safe in Chicago.

Natsuko: It is no longer safe anywhere.

Rosemary: At least for the moment, then.

Natsuko: Once the running starts it will never stop.

Rosemary: It'll all look different in Chicago. You'll have Mary and the baby.

Natsuko: My son-in-law is being shipped overseas. She is alone and frightened. She needs me.

Rosemary: Families should not be apart at a time like this.

Natsuko: Those who report will think I have considered myself better than they.

Rosemary: Just the one bag? I had you all packed.

Natsuko: Only what you can carry. I will not take more.

Rosemary: We didn't give in, Natsuko. We are not defeated.

Natsuko: There will be no end of shame.

Rosemary: Don't lose heart.

> *ROSEMARY goes to the back door.*

Lorraine! Linda! Harriet! It's time! (*To Sal*) Who is flying this plane of yours?

Sal: My cousin Tony.

Rosemary: He knows what he's doing?

Sal: Better than me.

> *HARRIET and LINDA come out of the house.*

Linda: Can I ride with them?

Rosemary: Absolutely not.

Harriet: What kind of plane is it?

Sal: Martin 130.

Harriet: China Clipper.

Sal: Customized. Beautiful.

Harriet: Luxury Liner in the sky. Four eight-hundred-fifty horsepower engines. Coast to coast is like fifteen, eighteen hours (*she snaps her fingers*) you're there.

Sal: Good for business.

Linda: Which business?

Sal: My father's business.

Linda: What business is that?

Sal: You still writin' that book?

Rosemary: Where's Lorraine? Lorraine!

> *LORRAINE comes out of the house carrying a suitcase.*

Sal: Beautiful.

Rosemary: What is the meaning of this?

Lorraine: It's what it looks like, Mother.

Sal: And they're off.

Linda: She's going with him. They're going to get married.

Harriet: Okay, deep breaths everyone. In. Out. Keep 'em coming.

Rosemary: You're not serious.

Lorraine: We'll send money.

> *SAL reaches into a pocket and pull*
> *out a fold of bills.*

Sal: Here, take it. Plenty where that came from.

> *SAL takes ROSEMARY'S hand an*
> *slaps the money into it.*

Rosemary: I am not for sale.

> *ROSEMARY drops the bills like*
> *something unclean.*

> *LINDA dives for them.*

Rosemary: You're not going anywhere.

Lorraine: Swift. Clean. It's the best way.

Rosemary: Take that suitcase and march back inside the house this instant.

Lorraine: You'll still have Harriet and Linda.

Rosemary: This is abandonment.

Lorraine: You're going to have to face this.

Rosemary: You don't love him. How could you?

Lorraine: I love him very much.

Linda: Two thousand dollars!

Harriet: You sure about this?

Lorraine: Yes.

Harriet: Because it's going to be hard to step back over the line once you've crossed it.

Lorraine: I'm sure.

Linda: I'd go in a minute.

ROSEMARY has to sit down.

Rosemary: What's going to become of us?

Linda: Can I?

Harriet: (*To Sal*) You'd better know what you're doing here, pal.

Sal: I'm going to take care of her.

Natsuko: I knew nothing good would come of this.

Rosemary: (*To Natsuko*) You *knew* about this.

Natsuko: No.

Lorraine: There is no one to blame.

Linda: I want to come!

Rosemary: *(To Natsuko)* Refuse to go. Make her listen.

Lorraine: I am going.

Natsuko: Now you would have me stay? What about *my* daughter?

Rosemary: Harriet, help me. Don't take them.

Harriet: She's right, Rose. Swift, clean. We can live through this. (*To Sal*) We need to go if we're going.

Sal: (*To Lorraine*) With us or without us, my father needs that plane in Chicago tomorrow.

Lorraine: (*To Rosemary*) It's not the end of the world.

Linda: Don't leave me here!

Rosemary: I'm begging you, Lorraine. Don't do this. Do I have to get on my knees?

Lorraine: Don't make this harder than it needs to be.

Rosemary: I will call the police! I will call the FBI! What you're doing is a federal crime, trying to help this stinking Jap escape! I will turn you in.

> *NATSUKO is not surprised by this*
> *betrayal.*

Harriet: All right, in the cab, now.

Rosemary: Better she should rot in prison than throw herself away.

Sal: You're wrong about me. Maybe one day you'll see that.

Rosemary: What about me? What happens to me?

Lorraine: You'll come visit.

Sal: Open invitation. Linda too.

> *LINDA runs into the house with the money.*

Linda: Don't leave without me. I'll be right back!

Rosemary: What am I going to do?

Lorraine: Try to be happy. I intend to be.

Harriet: Time for this train to leave the station. I'm going to pull the cab straight into my back yard. I'll give a little toot, you hustle over. Natsuko, you get in the back seat, hunker down out of sight, you got that?

Sal: Not a problem.

> *HARRIET hustles off to her yard.*

Rosemary: Natsuko, help me.

Natsuko: Gaman.

Rosemary: Someone. Please...

Natsuko: Gaman, to endure. It's what we do.

Sal: *(To Lorraine)* No regrets.

Lorraine: (*To Rosemary*) This isn't easy for me either.

Sal: Next stop, the rest of our lives.

Lorraine: You could help us both here.

Sal: Nothing else we can do, kiddo.

Natsuko: Now you must endure.

> *ROSEMARY and LORRAINE cannot*
> *break their connection.*

Rosemary: There's always something else to do.

Natsuko: To endure sorrow is always the last thing to be done.

> *HARRIET sounds her cab horn.*

Rosemary: (*Still on Lorraine*) I'm a disgrace.

> *NATSUKO takes a last look at*
> *her home.*

Natsuko: I doubt we will see each other again.

All eyes are on Natsuko.

No response.

NATSUKO exits.

Lorraine: Mother, please say goodbye.

Rosemary: You're no daughter of mine.

Lorraine: You're going to regret this.

Rosemary: I wouldn't count on that.

Lorraine: I'll call you.

Rosemary: I never want to hear from you again.

    Beat

    LORRAINE exits.

Sal: Wicked witch until the end, eh? Careful a house doesn't land on you. Might be your own.

Rosemary: Congratulations. You win. I lose.

Sal: Expect her call. We all win.

    SAL exits.

Rosemary: What have I done...? Lorraine.

> *LINDA runs out of the house with*
> *one arm in her coat sleeve, still*
> *trying to close her suitcase.*

Linda: Ready! Where'd everybody go?

Rosemary: You might as well march straight back to your room, young lady.

Linda: They left? (*Shouting*) Harriet! Come back!

Rosemary: And we'll have a thing or two to say about your betrayal later.

Linda: Come back!

> *LINDA collapses into tears.*

Rosemary: Sniveling excuse for a daughter.

> *LINDA escalates into a fit.*

All the tears in the world won't help us now.

> *LINDA charges into the house.*

> *We hear her shouting into the phone.*

Linda: Mrs. Wallace, Mrs. Wainwright, get off the line! I need to call the police! (*Beat*) I just do, that's why!

> *ROSEMARY goes in to intervene.*

Get off the line you old biddy hens! I need to report a crime!

Rosemary: Give me that phone. Thelma? Vi? Can you believe this child?

Linda: I hate you!

> *ROSEMARY comes back out onto the*
> *porch with the phone.*

It's nothing, just another one of our little tantrums.

> *LINDA comes to the doorway.*

Linda: You want to know what you are?

Rosemary: *(Into phone)* Hold on, girls. *(To Linda)* I am your mother, dear. At least we've always got that.

Linda: You're *ordinary*. Just like Lorraine.

> *LINDA goes inside, triumphant.*

ROSEMARY is devastated.

Beat

Rosemary: *(Into phone)* What? What's that? No, no, I'm keeping my distance from the likes of Natsuko Takimoto, believe me. (*Beat*) Exactly, the sooner the better. *(Beat)* I heard off the coast of Santa Barbara. *(Beat)* Oregon...when?

Black Out.

Eight

Scene:

Night. Abundant moonlight.

At Rise:

LORRAINE studies the moon with pragmatic curiosity more than out of winsome reverie. After a moment,

ROSEMARY opens the back door.

Rosemary: Linda, is that you?!

Lorraine: No and I'm never going to be either.

Rosemary: Oh. Lorraine.

Lorraine: Not to you anyway.

Rosemary: Where is Harriet?

Lorraine: Putting her cab in the garage.

Rosemary: I didn't think we'd see each other again.

Lorraine: That was Mary. Me, you didn't want to hear from.

Rosemary: This is all you have to offer, sarcasm? Ridicule?

Lorraine: Simple truth, Mother. I'm not like you. Not sarcasm. No ridicule.

Rosemary: You've come to your senses, then?

Lorraine: When I go, if I go, it won't be because I ran away.

Rosemary: In the end, he must have known he wasn't good enough for you.

Lorraine: In the *end*...I couldn't walk away from my responsibilities.

Rosemary: Obviously it wasn't the kind of love that could sustain a marriage.

Lorraine: We'll never know.

Rosemary: Was he decent about it?

Lorraine: Perfect gentleman.

Lights up on SAL.

Sal: Keep this up, kiddo, I'm going to need a neck brace.

Lorraine: …and my job, walk away without a word? No.

Sal: You deserve to be happy.

Lorraine: How am I going to be happy with out self-respect?

Sal: I'd like a shot at trying to make you happy.

Lorraine: And end up like my mother—no man, no confidence, no life? Is that what you want for me?

Sal: I'd give you anything you wanted.

Lorraine: Then let me have this. I had a moment of weakness, Sal. You've been so decent about everything.

Sal: You're sure?

Lorraine: As much as I can be. Will I kick myself tomorrow? I'll know tomorrow. Tonight I have to ask the unforgivable…again!

Sal: *(Beat)* I can't let you go thinking it's all you.

Lorraine: Don't try to make this easy for me. I've made a mess of it.

Sal: All my life I've been nothing but a bad joke.

Lorraine: Horribly selfish.

Sal: In the family, on the street.

Lorraine: It is not the time to be selfish.

Sal: I'm going to wait for you to listen. *(Beat)* You were right all along. Ask your sister…her friend Delores.

Lorraine: About what?

Sal: I've got to do this on my own or always wonder what I'm made of.

Lorraine: What's that got to do with Linda or Delores?

Sal: It gets down to where the school girls are laughing…time to stop kidding yourself.

Lorraine: You're going to do just fine.

Sal: I want to believe that.

Lorraine: Believe it. And be happy.

Sal: Could a grown old with you, kiddo.

Lorraine: I'd just as soon you didn't see me hairless, toothless, and riddled with varicose.

Sal: I'll never forget you.

Lorraine: I'll never forget you either.

Sal: Promise?

Lorraine: Promise.

> *They kiss.*

> *SAL exits.*

Rosemary: I promise never to mention it again.

Lorraine: Don't make promises you won't be able to keep.

Rosemary: It's a mystery where you get your strength.

Lorraine: From the moon. It has never let me down.

Rosemary: Your father's daughter, to be sure.

The moon occupies LORRAINE.

Lorraine: It's the gravitational pull that drags you back...holds you down. There's got to be some way to break free.

Rosemary: I would have been lost without you.

Lorraine: You tend to get what you want one way or another.

> *HARRIET enters with Lorraine's suitcase.*

Harriet: Forgot something.

Lorraine: Full moon tonight. Wasn't thinking.

Rosemary: Harriet, I've been out of my mind.

Harriet: I gather you didn't call the police.

Rosemary: Linda has run off.

Lorraine: What happened?

Rosemary: She hates me.

Lorraine: She hates everyone. She'll be back.

Rosemary: She said we were *ordinary*.

Harriet: She's young yet.

Lorraine: She's probably at Delores's.

Rosemary: No, I called. She's not there.

Lorraine: Was Delores there?

Rosemary: Yes. She knows nothing.

Harriet: She can't have gone far.

Rosemary: She has all that filthy money. Two thousand dollars. I wasn't paying attention.

Harriet: I'll get the cab out. Don't worry, I won't come home without her.

HARRIET exits to her yard.

Rosemary: (*Despairing*) She's gone.

Lorraine: If that's true, you're going to have to survive it. We're not going to go back to where we were.

Rosemary: No, we can't go back. The woman I thought I might become...never had a chance.

Lorraine: Do you think we'll ever get there, the moon?

Rosemary: I think there's a greater chance of that than of our ever seeing Linda again.

Lorraine: (*Of the moon*) I think we will.

Rosemary: You and your moon. Where's Lorraine? Where is she? Where is that girl? Check the yard. There's a harvest moon tonight...blue moon tonight...forever wishing on the moon. (*Of Linda's return*) I'm afraid to hope. (*Beat*) There's a chill in the air. I'm going in.

> *ROSEMARY takes Lorraine's suitcase and goes inside, a woman older than her years.*

> *LORRAINE bathes in the moonlight. She heads inside stopping on a porch step for one last glance at the moon.*

Lorraine: I think we're going to figure out a way.

> *LORRAINE exits into the house.*

> *Curtain.*

Breinigsville, PA USA
22 February 2011
256155BV00001B/1/P